LOOK AT LIFE

WORDS FROM MY HEAD
VOLUME 3

After years in the automotive business, in and around the United States, I moved to the desert of Southern Utah.

It was in early 2018 where the red rocks of the area inspired some hidden creativity.

I started to write poetry. I had a goal to write one poem every day, with a serious wonder if it could be done, at least by me.

Well, almost four years later, and close to 800 poems, rants, thoughts, and crazy words have been written.

Who would have thought that an old Harley riding, mountain biking, serious powder, and mogel skier had any creative juices inside his head?

I hope you enjoy my thoughts and get some mind fulfillment reading my words linked together to form these books.

Thank You;

Look at Life

Words from My Head
Volume 3

by

Brian Hill

AELIN PUBLISHERS
India

Published by Aelin Publishers India

This is a work of fiction. Names, characters, places, businesses, and incidents are products of the author's imagination or used in a fictitious manner. Any resemblance to any actual person, living or dead, events or locales is entirely coincidental.

ISBN 978-93-92316-19-7

www.aelinpublishers.com
Email: aelinpublishers@gmail.com
Instagram/Twitter: aelinpublishers

it’s Thanksgiving day in a year that sucked
we haven't had fun, in that you can trust
it's really about over, and we all need to cheer
2020 is behind and absolutely will disappear
be thankful for the doctors, scientists, and all
be thankful for tomorrow and hope you don't fall
be careful, have some fun, wear a mask like you should
give this year the middle finger and good-riddance for good....

tomorrows the future, let's hope that it's bright
it could be worse, and that thoughts a fright
think good thoughts today and tomorrow will be
a brighter and happier time, you'll see....

the world has been messed up, I'm sure you can agree
you wake up, you get up, and face it, “on three”
you have to stay honest if you're going to prevail
it's set up in such a crazy way, and very easy to fail
make sure to have your coffee, before you venture out
it gives you a shot, to move ahead, without a single doubt
take on this world, that has gone mad, take it on and kicks its ass
you'll be surprised what you can do, and do it with great class....

the disappearance of beauty is happening
will tomorrow give us a magnificent experience
an occurrence not like today
episodes of normal that we once celebrated
let's cherish memories and hope
possibilities will breathe new beauty into our days....

"let death be what take us, not lack of imagination"
BJ Miller said this in his Ted Talk
(What really matters at the end of life)
profound truth with honesty that has been hidden lately
after hearing it I knew I had to share it....

got a call from my head and it told me to accept
it's not often you get this kind of call
confusing and harsh as the thought was, I listened
I listened to the sound that only one's head, can have
slow down, the world will follow
seek others point of view
believe that two ideas can be different, but equal
understand, listen, process, and be....

you seem surprised to hear from me
things came up we just didn't see
how can it be that we both had the notion
to relive the past and find old devotion
talking with you brightened up my day
to think about things that had just slipped away
old times relived, seem so simple I know
but that's just not the truth, as memories just go
this is a message to all of us out there
reach out to the ones whose lives we once shared
thanks to you all who have read what I have penned
in the name of our memories, and of course, good friends....

happiness starts in someone's eyes
by what we see and how we surmise
goes right to our soul by way of good thoughts
and it's no surprise that thoughts call the shots
sometimes it turns those thoughts into actions
and your day evolves into a pleasant distraction
amen....

amazingly, the wonder of patience is lost
it doesn't want to be found, it seems at any cost
when we were young and so carefree we paid no never-mind
we rode our bikes, we played hopscotch, and mostly never whined
what are your thoughts as to who is lost and the reasons why it's so
it is too late, have we waited too long and do we really want to know....

blackbirds flying at night are unseen
unseen by the human eye, lost in a cloak of darkness
lost till dawn, they may fly without human distress
fly in the gift of darkness without any concern
wait, do birds fly at night
never seen one....

cavities in our mind create chambers for thought
it starts with just one, but without it, their naught
thoughts are productive and need to be wooed
gather all from the chamber, then submit for review
hold on to the good ones and cast out the rest
someday in the future, they could be addressed....

understand the strength and stability "of now"
live not in the past, for the future
take the moment "of now" and develop
take those "now seconds" turn them into well-done actions...

where is humanity hiding
what have they done with the rules
who was in the room while deciding
it must have been a room full of fools
humanity is understanding and compassion
something we've had all along
whoever hid it, is an assassin
they hid something we need and that's wrong
we will uncover humanity
we'll find where it's hidden away
we need to shut down this calamity
I believe we need do it TODAY...

magnificently beautiful, the newborn laughed
laughing out loud for the horde to hear
this horde had been waiting for decades for this birth
waiting and wondering and marveling at what was to come
and now, it has been birthed
the release of the future is now present...

as the world turns, so do the minds of life
life will move forward preserving itself
will mankind be included
of course, you say, however...
mankind will be the reason that preservation is necessary....

living, loving, dancing, and creating are the simple things we have
live today and live tomorrow in the best way possible
don't waste the time you exist by living it in fear
learn the reasons for your fear and conquer them
find truth in what you don't recognize "as truth"
there is always 2 sides to the situation....

conversations in my head sound like this
sssssssssssssssssssssssssssss
I don't know how any thoughts find there way out
ssssssssssssssssssssssss—oooooooo
wait, did you hear that change up
yep, that's a thought...!

silent stupor and useless disorder are soon to be led off a cliff
as in any crazy cycle, the remains of many will be the only proof
proof that mankind is subject to political, chemical and social viruses
but really, all in the same year.... FU*k...

the walls began to open
the sights are coming in
it's as if the world is broken
and leaving us all to spin
it appears to be neglected
it needs some love real fast
mankind needs to be directed
so, we will not be the last
the struggle is now beginning
let's see it through to the end
we can do this, let’s all start winning
let's get this world on the mend....

the ghost shouted the solution to all that would believe
not any of the living, had the wherewithal to perceive
what has gone wrong with this cycle, what has taken all control
are we abandoned by our history, are we stuck in a giant hole
do we realize who the ghost is, are we ready with open eyes
listen careful to the history, the future will not be a surprise....

the precision of nature we depend on, we hope it never disappoints
this time of the year the solstice is here, and winter, it anoints
our time in the light gets shorter, until the arrival of this great event
the days are instantly longer as the Sun does what it is meant
it welcomes in a new season and says goodbye to the past
the days get brighter and longer and with that, yesterday is caste....

nothing displeases silence as quickly as the noise
I know this sounds, literally crazy, as I try to regain poise
my mind was reduced to simple thoughts as I opened up from sleep
sometimes I know, my brain just goes, with words that are too deep...!

in the depth of today's disturbance, there is an escape
the overwhelming evidence is in the art of discovery
learning how wrong or how right you are by the intoxicating evidence
evidence, that both sides seem to have and believe
that my friends is where a disturbance dwells
in the mirror you will greet the only someone that can change the outcome....

isn't it almost impossible to believe that 2020 was real
I just want it to move forward and allow us to see it in the rearview
see it, feel it, and forget it
is that even possible, I mean, the forget part
never forget that such human separation by crazy, uncaring leadership can happen
let's remember the wonderful people that put heir lives on the line
they were there daily helping and caring for the sick
finding ways to lessen the blow of the insane virus
let's celebrate the Holiday Season and welcome in the New Year
celebrate with LOVE, COMPASSION, KINDNESS, and FORGIVENESS
thank you for the year I had and thank you for the friends that shared it....

today is the day that we all celebrate for our own special reasons
be grateful, be appreciative, be humble, most mostly be alive
be alive with the spirit of all that is right and good for YOU
be humble and respect the idea and beliefs of others
but again, be excited to be living in a time where so many choices exist
bless you, all and happy holidays....

illusions, all strong illusions
with watery eyes and smokey air, everything seems illusionistic
waking from the deepest sleep
a deep sleep of my lost eternity and it's frightening
can, or could you, see past the forgotten life of sanity
wake up in the proper time warp and believe what you've seen
or not and take the easy way....

where do you want to go, where do you want to be
close your eyes, think deep inside, and off you go, you'll see
no matter what direction, boundaries are just not there
all you do is think and feel, then escape, into thin air
if it's not a place that fills your mind, it's a color or book you see
do the very same just change the name, the effects will set you free....

magnetism, imaginary or real
definition - a physical phenomenon produced by
the motion of electric charge...
resulting - attractive and repulsive forces
between objects
anything here sound like our political system today
asking for a friend....

the incident that happened is a telling event
the leader in the seat is filled with contempt
he knows that real soon his days are "very" through
the nation is over his presiding over coups
people can't be patriots and survive behind him
it's time to believe, his direction is simply grim....

bring on our new day
experience the waking of dawn
raw newness being born of night sky magic
yawning and reaching for that very enchanted moment
pausing only for reality to achieve its arising
following this occurrence, a new day may proceed....

surrounded by the desert and continuous natural grandeur
make me a freak of nature and somewhat of a voyeur
the sights and formations aplenty, are enough to boggle your eyes
what you see and where it happens is constantly a surprise
even clouds are different, in the hot dry desert air
welcome to the desert, you will never be bored, I swear....

two people often, don't actually agree
life is like that, and I think it's key
it happens in aspects of everyone's life
religious, political, or just options, give strife
know how to summon all meaningful things
agree to disagree and see what it brings
life is too precious to exist with contempt
get along with your neighbors, or at least, just attempt....

mother earth, she dreams in color
she desired to be left alone
it started out strong, than man came along
with discoveries advancing the unknown
mother earth was fine with volcanos
dark clouds, lighting and rain
then life shows up and needs a cup
to hold man, who craved, all-terrain
what to do, mother earth cried, with thunder
could she and mankind make a team
well, mankind prevailed and evolved quite fast
and accomplished one hell of a dream....

someone said "good morning"
I listened
someone said "have a nice day"
I listened
someone said "you look nice today"
I listened
someone said "have a good night"
I listened
someone said "what a great time to be alive"
we should all listen....

as I look back on current events
timing requires a little common sense
oh my God, for the chaos, with life here on earth
from where I sit now, it needs a REBIRTH
what should we do, all ye fellow earthlings
do we wait while others continue to stir things...?

the view from here is my salvation
how I got here needs explanation
again, from this view, you can watch from afar
getting up here, you just wish on a star
starlight, star bright, the first star you see
say it once with real meaning and behold where you'll be....

look within yourself
search for your kindness, you know it's there
find ways to respect and share
keep the negativity under control
love and honor with truthful actions
oh wow, these thoughts were on my mind as I awoke
does this mean I'm woke?...

as the words escaped from their hidden space
their meanings were free and open to embrace
as they descended from the keeper of words
they had to decide if they were nouns or verbs
take just a minute and try to understand
language is different and tough to command
some words in English, sound just the same
THEIR objective is THERE and THEY'RE quite the word game....

listen to the quite of your mind
dream so you can feel your imagination
dream and reach above
dream and exist outside of yourself
fantasize your very existence,
escape reality without leaving the room
dream big, fly high, go far, return by clicking your shoes....

attention, attention everyone
ding, dong, hi ho, and merry ooooo
the crazy orange one is gone....

the dark, vapor filled cloud, drifted over the peak
drifted over for all to see what is about to happen
life-giving moisture was about to pay a visit to the desert
with a lighting flash, followed by a thunderous boom, it began
what a relief....

what happens, as we concentrate on 'what's happening'
I seem to have a question living somewhere inside my mind
living in the folds of my vast memories wondering what's happening...?

it happened suddenly with a raw, real, and alarming quickness
a thought, an idea, or maybe even an understanding
yeah, it was scary
I now know, or understand, and perhaps appreciate
oh shit, I get it...!

it stormed last night with snow al-la-mode
covering the trees with way too much load
storms have a way of being a bit scary
dropping so much, earth and trees cannot carry
trees try to bend and allow for the weight
earth drinks it up, till it hits its full state
nature has a way to fill its own glass
man has to wait, sit back, and let it pass....

what do you feel, when you close your eyes
do you see the world, in an odd, unique size
how do feel, when someone says they care
can you feel the passion when they are not there
open your eyes and see what is true
experience the frontier, that is offered to you....

as the future unfolds in front of itself, I wonder
I wonder what emotions will rise from within
from within hidden voids of my mind
the very mind, that in the past, was open to shifts
shifts in all areas of my thinking and realizations
areas that I thought existed together harmoniously
no, they exist only in separate vacancies, within themselves
look forward into these vacancies
are they in focus...

what do you see in the mirror today
who is staring back when you do
is the reflection the same as it was before
or a different and varied point of view
face the facts, we've all had to change
what you see in the mirror, is you
let's hope you like the reflection you see
or is a shift, something you must do...?

there are conflict and confusion behind the door
do we keep the door shut and stay in the fantasy
or....

my heart has discovered you
the very deepest, most genuine, of you
what do assume was felt
I cannot betray what is....

the shadows in your view have to be there for reasons
what is it
where is the light coming from that cast the shadow
what does the shadow represent
can you tell....

light easily occurs between the cracks in the void
living, breathing, open cracks
opened by the wish or desire to learn
longing for the vast knowledge that is there
see it, feel it, catch it
become creative and find your silver lining....

alone and touched
can you feel the caress
feel it deep within
charged, changed, or transformed
feel it deep within....

do you feel your mind closing your choices
choices are the options, that are, or we're, your only alliance within
within the inner portions of self-guidance and guilt
is your guilt guiding your mind to un-felt emotions
OMG, where is this coming from and going?
MY MIND NEEDS TO BE CLOSED, for TODAY...!

today is yesterdays tomorrow
did you think it would come so fast
how did you plan your future
were you aware, it had been cast
what you do today is history
as tomorrow becomes today
after all, yesterday, you were busy
do you think what you did was passe...?

I wanted myself to want this
I wanted this more than anything
more than anything I've ever wanted
why was wanting this so impossible
what part of it shakes me to my core
it's such a little desire
tiny in fact
oh, crap, WTF, and sh@t
eat your damn cake...!

a day without being able, to do
what is YOUR, to do?
have you done it before?
has the present world climate added to your to do list
think about it, make your list and see....

it's very clear that in life we don't always get what we want
planning and planning sometimes just goes wrong
the super bowl of living always has a winner
it just may not be me....

there's always time to see, through all the crazy haze
if you take the time to look, it only takes a gaze
what you see may be amazing, or nothing there at all
your point of view is vital before you make the call
take the time to see it, to open up your view
you have to see and feel it, and then you have a clue....

my thoughts, surrounding my thoughts, were misunderstood
I was deeply troubled by the controversies brought into view
I did not recognize the reasons
why and how we're added to the confusion
how do you know when to believe
how do you know you were mistaken...?

there is a place where it all started
no-one knows why the clouds all parted
whoever was looking, got the best view by far
seeing was believing, as the sky went bizarre
clouds took on a very strange shape
the winds took hold and let nothing escape
down it can with a thunderous thud
crazy as it sounds, it was pelting out mud
it only last, a second or two
(wait, my mind just wandered off with
a strange poem idea, what were you saying)....?

lookup -- see what's aloft
imagine - magical beasts living above
living within the transparency of a vast, empty sky
the emptiness that was trivial until the sightings
sightings seen drifting in the vastness of the above-mentioned
help the magical creatures develop a presence in a story
a story untold for millions of years
and then you ---
you looked up....

what I saw yesterday, created by mother nature, just blew me away
mounds of earth, shape shifting with the weather
changing every time rain falls and wind blows
slowly and constantly, with the natural brush strokes from mother
earthly wonders are, well, a WONDER...!

lips kiss, fingers touch
eyes see, oh so much
ears listen, to the sounds of the day
skin covers, your soul on display
arms are for holding, the ones that you adore
legs give you balance, to get out there and explore
they said it wouldn't be easy, learning to live and love while here
use everything you're born with, use it all, and have no fear....

what time have you got, we asked the young man
he looked at us both and then he began
without hesitation, he spoke and he said
a "half-hour ago" and then shook his head
my laugh came out quickly as I said with a smile
I love that great answer it's got some fun style
may I use that answer when asked for the time
he laughed and he said "yep" for a dime....

elevate and study the delicate opinions of the world
are they for you to believe and understand
are they for you to accept and utilize
are they what you want in your life everyday
you have the power to decide
only you, for you, has that kind of power and energy
USE IT....

what is it about, the tambourine
you shake it like crazy, it's never serene
a circle of wood or some other thing
lots of little metal cymbals that strike with a ring
it's a funny little device with no real purpose
you bang it on stuff to keep it in service
who would have thought, it could be so essential
the fact here is, everything has potential....

too much
too little
too few
too soon
why does it seem like that
why does asking this question seem so hard
I don't know
I don't understand
I don't really care
what happened to us
what happened to the joy
what happened
asking for a friend...!

before I seek the answer
I must provide the question
before either, I must yearn
I must choose to reach for knowledge
I must....

ladders are involved in life
climb into personal gateways
up and down into opportunities as they occur
weeping and smiling during the experience
don't miss a step during the venture
enjoy all that your ladder will introduce....
the dark and forgotten face of time
time that was in a bottle
a time, with too much time on my hands
when a moment in time meant something
that time we all had the time of our lives
I want to get back to old time rock and roll
as time goes by one last time, because
I haven't got time for the pain
let's dance, like it feels, like the first time....

weeping and lost
my mind has been squashed
so confused and annoyed
I need me some Freud
I'm really just rambling
till the words come a scrambling
wait, the coffee is done
let's now have some fun....

I walked into my memory of the not too distant past
sounds giving rise to long-forgotten thoughts
engines of aircraft flying above in early morning air
outcries of cars, screening along the near freeway
quacking ducks and honking geese, swimming in the trailside river
the old neighborhood is so the same, but different
remembering the past with fond thoughts
being happy with the change and accepting closure....

can I go the distance, can I stay in the game
will I need assistance, can I make my claim
I will start at the beginning, I will go to the end
I'm sure I'll be grinning, that's what I intend
that wasn't so tough, I made it look easy
I thought it'd be rough, I did get a bit wheezy
it tells me I CAN, and so CAN you
startup with, I began, and then just follow-through....

all heads turned towards the first useful prophecy
information was streaming into the skulls of the masses
the most distinguished will retain only a small info-bit
can we move forward when the empty heads are full
can we...?

I hate to always exaggerate, so why not just collaborate
let's see how it navigates, before it can contaminate
I know that at this rapid rate, the problem will refrigerate
what is this thing I orchestrate, let's move it to a latter date
I'm done with trying to agitate, isn't it time to graduate...?

are you willing to see magic
is it in each of us, to decide what is magic
my magic, not your magic, not their magic
the moon, as it reflects its magic to your eye
is it your eye, the reflection, or the moon itself
the desert cactus growing, without water, and blooming
where is the magic there
dogs, as they gaze at you with those eyes
I love my personal magic world
magic, is a surrounding enchantment, to be beheld....

it's rather surprising, they laughed
how could something, so extraordinary, be so
be so what, was the question all through the land
yes, it was seen and felt everywhere
how could that be
be so what, is still the question
so simple, so beautiful, so dangerous
the answer is this
you decide, then you tell us....

the depth of touch
the sparkle in the soul
takes on what life gives out
makes it seem so whole
share it if you can
pass along the glow
don't keep it for yourself
help others to plateau....

it's complicated he said
what I see, and the way I see it is complicated
how is that so, I asked
I did not understand
how is seeing or hearing the same thing, viewed so different
this question will topple worlds....

can't we pretend we are back in time
where things were easy and not a crime
when that was that and this was this
not like now, where it seems all amiss
I for one think, looking back is fun
I'm not like some, who want it undone
learn from the past, we are now in the present
what's done is over, it wasn't all really pleasant
leave it alone, understand, the past is the past
times and beliefs were different and life wasn't as fast
I know that some readers will have different thoughts
that's ok, I'm sure, but please don't be cross....

join me as I transport myself into my mind
I will guide you, with a bit of a scare, I'm sure
be careful, as I leap into a void of confusion
confusion, that started at the origin, and has been building since
are you with me
do you feel your thoughts getting scrambled
scrambled while we travel on the road paved with confusion
wait... "I'm confused", the road is now gone
we have been set in motion, we are forever lost in thought
we can only think our way out
I think I can, I think I can, I think I can
do you think you can
welcome back, confused travelers....

is it possible, that you crossed over to the void
experiences, to other regions of the mind, need to be studied
how is that done when it happens, unseen and unknown
well, funny you should ask
it must be studied
how, (asking for a friend)
I think there is a need.... 🤪

who's the manipulators standing in the crowd
the ones in back or the ones that are loud
it's hard to know when their both so confused
they both want whats theirs and think they're abused
what I want, and YOU want, are completely the same
I want MY rights to be valued, BUT please play MY game
YOU wish to inform me, that I am SO wrong
but YOUR way is wrong, and YOU just don't belong
it's been this WAY since the birth of mankind
WE should think, that at some time, a truth, "WE WILL FIND"...

the voice of the young
needs to learn to survive
the voice of the young
are needing to thrive
the voice of the young
need to stand up and shout
the voice of the young
are the future no doubt
without the strength, of the young
does the future exist
without the strength of the young
we all, are just mist....

the world dreams in shadows brought on by the night
color comes to the mind during memory waves
think back to the time you first experienced a sunset
a coloring splash, transforming everything you knew before
that's a memory wave....

the middle of the room was filled with randomness
why the middle you ask
answer is this
you have to have random so you can plan normalcy
plus, it allows me to use these words together
serious brainstorming this morning....

there are exceptional aspects of our world that are surprising
facts of life, that go beyond the norm, known by most
we all have a fascination when we get the chance to witness
like, seeing a mating pair of hawks, doing their daredevil air dance
breaking all flight barriers to share in their idea of "Life Flight"
it was a wonderful sighting....

around the porch light, before it was turned off, you could see them
the soft glow of fluttering wings
hundreds of lively, tiny, critters
nighttime beasts, that gather at light sources, to mingle among others
where do they come from, where do they go
silly questions that need answers
don't they...?

who remembered the unknown clairvoyant
how did it happen, was there enjoyment
have to say this, they probably knew
saw it all coming in good ole plain view
being a clairvoyant, I'm sure isn't easy
seeing what's coming can make one quite queasy
today's words are disjointed, I really must confess
not sure, at all how, this poem turned to mess
but writers will know, when your brains spill some shit
you keep on keeping on, till it tells you to quit
I quit....!

suddenly a thought came to me
why
it's not something I ever wanted or even thought about
what is going on
cricket, really (been watching too much UK TV)
you gotta watch out for random thoughts....

love is and love floats
love gives and love gloats
love finds and then loves takes
love's kind, and love will break
love's choice but love's selective
love's rejoice, love's effective
love exists, but love can fade
love twists, when love is made
love is alive and love is dead
find your love and lose your head
love has all this and so much more
we all need love, mi Amor....

what is trendy for you today
is it cool to learn what's really okay
what do you do when someone is hassled
do you sit there quiet and become tasseled
it's tough today to get involved
the problem is big and needs to be solved
the year gone by, showed us all we need work
it got so bad, I admit went beserk
I'm trying hard to learn what's okay
let's all try harder, let's make it today....

why won't you listen
pay attention to me please
you need to listen....

place yourself where believing is natural
what do you see, how do you feel
what is different, was it necessary
do you believe this place exists outside the mind
will you come back...?

put yourself in their place
what do you see from inside that space
how do you feel about their point of view
can you understand why they do what they do
are you seeing the world from the left or the right
is what you see in black or in white
understand this, both views are not wrong
we see what we see, so let's all get along....

lookup to the sky
see what wasn't there before
the ever-changing vastness of possibilities
how small and insignificant our understanding is
how can we compare what we see to what we realize
lookup and see what has been rewritten....

where does your face end
look into the mirror and see
the mirror is one way
where does it end....

I'm skipping today
too much going on to write
I'll write tomorrow....

to know the answers is a power in itself
to know the question is even more valuable
here exists, what I believe, is the only unanswered question
who let the dog out
or maybe this
who asked the first question and
did they know, it was a question...?

early morning - it begins
noon - it continues
afternoon - it slows down
evening - it's ending
night time - call it done
days of our life....

morning - welcome yourself into the day
afternoon - get stuff done
evening - look back, reflect, have some wine
night - relax your body, mind, spirit, and....

look into the cool waters of life
what you see is a constant moving of memories
past happenings that have connected your existence
these connections have gathered together in rhythm
an in-sync reminder, to you, of what has been....

befallen with misfortune
wandering within the time warp
bumping into lost sightings of the forgotten
surfing the waves of distraction and amusement
(and now a word from our sponsor
how's your morning going before coffee)...?

needing to know is not the same
understanding the need materializes out of fascination
developing that desire could influence the mind to perform
oh, but for the need for more data...!

the human song started with fire
fire gave rise to so much more than flame
so much more than protection
much more than food
fire turned the nomad man into modern man
fire was the turning point for us....

sometimes the silence interrupts the quiet
absence of all noise is a nuisance to the mind
we need disturbance to accept reality
yore tells us that man cannot be sociable in stillness....

believing in others before yourself can produce anxiety
learn from the success of the ones you are hearing
self-esteem and self-awareness are the secret sauce
find your sauce and you will discover yourself....

the hows and whys of mankind becoming modern was and is fascinating
in thousands of year's we have been through a vast amount of stages
one would think that repeating mistakes would not be one of them
well, wrong, wrong, wrong
I hope that future generations of humans will get it right....

the language of poetry lives within your senses
sight, sound, smell, taste, and touch
you must feel the harmony and understand their process
sometimes the sixth sense visits and awareness becomes clearer....

don't forget to remember yourself
the you's in the world, keep us all on the shelf
let's not forget how you stole all my love
carried me along, through the skies up above
showed me how to be, the one that I am
gave me wings to reach as high as I can
don't forget to remember, the you, I adore
as we glide through this life and continue to explore....

behold the morning light and know that it has begun
the beginning, is in cycle
this process has never been different or ever altered
is it a procedure that needs improving
does it require man to exploit it for his satisfaction
I think not
the natural beauty, of the beginning, is perfect as it IS....

wait, please wait
I'm falling behind
I’ve never been here
it’s so undefined
I can't understand it
the view is so varied
what to do, what to do
I feel so, so harried
it's quite unusual
for me to be here
it's a simple reaction
but I'm standing in the rear....

as we walk the earth we realize its birth
as we breathe the air we know we are there
as we wake in the morn we are truly re-born
as we observe the sights take time to delight
life here in this world takes time to unfurl
take the time that you need so you can succeed
we are all in this space let's live it in grace
as we walk on this earth let us value our birth....

sensitive words are experienced by different minds
letters thrown together to create the event
poets, authors, novelists, playwrights, screenwriters
organizing words in different ways
creating numerous magical patterns
patterns of which you, the recipient, are the benefactor....

how do you know if you are you
what if in fact, your not the you, you knew
how did the change happen and when was it so
memories remained but the looks had to go
gray hair and bad gas were not things back then
it happened quite slow and then it happened again
what to do, what to do, about this crazy change
if we could, could we ask, for a whole rearrange....

breathe in life each day
take that moment to relive that last second
think about others reliving at the same moment
how can something so simple be so fundamental....

come to the fair and have a drink
the hillbilly highball will make you think
the hillbilly highball is a wonderful thing
I've heard lots of tales and lots of folks sing
no one remembers the taste or the smell
some say that their journey was straight into hell
others believe that they really could fly
they probably did but didn't know why
the hillbilly highball is fuel for the mind
not sure how it happens but it just unwinds
notllo sure what it's made of, but it can't be good
for all we know, it's piss and some wood
the highbilly highball is a wonderful drink
you stop, drop, and takeoff, then totally sink....

listen carefully to the sounds of the mind
pulling and stretching, thoughts from behind
taking what's real and replacing with dreams
fantasies galore and stories unseen
don't be fearful of the sounds in your head
learn what exists, just don't be misled
(not at all sure how these words came to be
the sounds in my mind were provoking me....)

there are lovely, unstated words, departing from my mind
soft and inspiring, slipping out from behind
I have very little control over these tiny creative quirks
as if they have been hiding and warming in the works
I often used to wonder where all the words all came from
but I gave it up to let them out and beat their very own drum....

among us - there are extraordinary things
creatures taken for granted by all us human beings
look at the butterfly and follow his life trail
from an crazy ugly caterpillar to a beautiful swallowtail
snakes are something that most don't understand
how do they move so quickly is the question in demand
simple creatures like ants are the community in a hole
workers, hunters, and the queen, all have an intended role
as the top of the animal kingdom, we need to understand
we share the world with all life here, let's honor it while we can....

is it an accident that we go around
we go around as if we are bound
around the sun, around the block
around and around, and around the clock
it's dizzying to think of the many times
we've spun around to avoid the climb
round and around and around we go
where will it stop, do we want to know....

who is to blame, does it require shame
did you just forget, bring on the regret
will you try to remember, and temper your temper
again and again, you better find ZEN....

somewhat blankly, the number drowned the facts
what facts you ask
doesn't matter
you wouldn't believe them anyway....

life will surely be good fortune for you
follow your heart into the unfamiliar and find it
it is there for all to discover
it is there hidden in plain sight
do not close your mind to the ease of the search....

how do you know, what you know, when you know
how did you find what you found
was the hill really up, was the house down the street
did the river fill with water on it's own
sand is sandy, dirt is dirty, and mud is dirt that is wet
water that's hard is considered to be ice
but hot, it appears to be steam
why did you imagine the earth to be round
and space, the final frontier
how did you know, you knew, what you knew
when what you knew, was so extremely, extreme....

waking and walking into your own innocent eyes
seeing what was neglected for years
comprehending this space, for the first time
being receptive to the abandoned awareness of your reality....

to recognize reality, you must understand, the reality
reality is subject to interpretation and the viewpoint of, what is out
what, is not always, what is....

the silence in my mind was disturbed by the rushing of blood
pounding the inner ear with unpleasantness
stirring silent thoughts of sleep, that would not come
I must quiet the silence
I must wake from the unpleasant pounding
I must wake up to unravel the disturbance....

contain your entire self in the box of life
pour some liquid emotion on it and COVER it
step back and see if your view has transformed
now, I mean now, yes, NOW
do you feel the warmth that overflowed your mind
if not, you could still be asleep....

with perfect shades of light
we bid farewell to the night
breathe deep for the lingering soul
about to lose all control
gather all the energy within
to face the dawning again
the dusk is about to change
to an essence that is steady and strange....

is it what you want, is it what you need
is it what you thought, is it guaranteed
what is your wish, what is your desire
is it love, is it hate, will it help you to reach higher
what is it that you dream about, what is it that you
wish
why oh why is it in your head, after all, your just a
fish....

time is measured in countless moments
how you use them is simply a component
decisions reflect in all directions
make the right one and seek no corrections
can you see that time is shared by all
achieve all the moments, the big and the small....

the dotted line is never longer than it should be
how long or short is always going to surprise
do not be afraid of the dots
do not be afraid of the length
no circumstance regarding dots should be ignored
search for your dotted line and advance....

I work for the man to earn my bread
I work for the man to keep me fed
I work for my God to understand
I work for myself to get the upper hand
I live my life in a world that's cold
I live my life and I just grow old
I live my life with assorted rules
I live my life in a world that's cruel
I play sometimes to set myself straight
I play sometimes so I don't have to hate
I play with intensity to gain respect
I play so hard so I don't forget
I know in life we all must die
I know it's for sure so I often cry
I know we all started out the same
I know our life is a prolonged game
I want to be everything I can
but remember to live, I work for the man
I do it with love for the ones I hold close
I do it for me, and for me it's grandiose....

movements and rambles through life should be fun
taking the time to have your eyes opened
liberated to the concept of, WTF was that
you might be a tiny bit astounded by it....

have fun in the present, wait for the rest
be worthy to be there and be at your best
does it really matter if you win or not
what makes a difference is you gave it that shot....

trying to be, who you are is hard
spending time with yourself will put you on guard
being The Who, that you have become
will bore or excite, but do not succumb
it's taken some time to build the real you
spend the time that you need to see the task
through....

follow today's path
take on your unique journey
pursue it all day....

the skills of a few
are they limited to the few
do those few know they are the few
are those few aware of their skill...?

lost in my own mind
being aware of the dark
adjusting is slow....

I know I'm gunna do it
you know I'm gunna do it
so I do it....

remember to remember
it is that time of year
remember those that left their mark
cry a couple of tears....

the joys of the world, are purely delicious
to find them you may, have to be ambitious
instead of struggling, all about your day
open your eyes and behold, what's behind all the haze
as surprising as it is, it's really not hard
the world is wide open and is your back yard....

water, water, wherefore are thou
rivers are shallow and lakes need help now
find us please and save the terrain
send us clouds filled with lots of rain
send in the storms that will refresh the lands
send in the thunder with the clap of your hands
rain on us now before we forget
rain on us please and let us get wet
we need the water to refresh the earth
we need the rain to give us rebirth....

there are shadows lurking
are they following or leading
are there answers...?

it was an early dream
a dark visitor appeared in my mind
what message is being delivered
who is this dark visitor
why is this visit so powerful
open your mind
listen to the voice
that's all you can do....

will tomorrow survive today
will today turn the future into reality
what is the truth and who will tell us
do we understand how and why it will be
revealed....

where does today fit into your future
are you going to let it unravel itself
do you see yourself challenging the pathway
go where YOU want, not where IT wants....

I felt dizzy with excitement as I realized the end
was near
the climb sucked the breath out of me
every pedal, push, and pull became an achievement
what was I thinking....?

there is always the other decision
whoops, did I say that....?

I've been on this journey since I don't know when
I do know, it's been long, but I'd do it again
I've learned and I've squirmed as I've sauntered this road
there's been roadblocks and high peaks and sunrises that glowed
I'm convinced that our journeys are endless in desire
the fact is, I'm sure, it's how we reach higher
journey with someone so the experience is shared
share the ups and the downs and all roadblocks when scared
take on your life's journey, take it on till complete
all journeys are different and certainly unique....

the irritated look suddenly became the norm
people walking around with a blank stare
starting at emptiness and uncertainty
what and why has this emerged
cycle, climate, ignorance, or just bad coffee....?

the knowledge, the universe holds, is precious
what is out there, what waits in the darkness
what can humans comprehend and value
is that the question we need to be answered...?

calculated risk
estimated conclusions
desired outcomes...?

the power and of nature is a beautiful thing to behold
to see and smell what is created within the earth, is a worthy destination
fires destroy and cleanse, and with that, provide room for regeneration
Ah, but for being out mingling, with Mother Nature....

you can walk the streets of "Everywhere"
in your mind, you can stroll to places no one has been or seen
exciting and peaceful at the same time, as running with bulls
take time to go somewhere near "Everywhere"....

the morning is cloudy with a very slight breeze
wishing and hoping that it lowers the degrees
the heat has been torturous all around the land
it's nice to have it cooler as the warmth is out of hand
here's hoping that the heat will not be here very long
the weather patterns are crazy and just do not belong....

I'm wandering through my memories and it's harder than you think
how old was I when this took place and why is everything pink
I remember this and remember that, but it's all a whirling haze
my mind is spinning around and around, in this crazy memory maze
you would think that memories would be easy, but it's really not the case
wandering through this place, that is your mind, is equal to walking in space....

thank you

www.ingramcontent.com/pod-product-compliance
Lightning Source LLC
LaVergne TN
LVHW090133160826
845673LV00017B/2456

* 9 7 8 9 3 9 2 3 1 6 1 9 7 *